THE WESTMINSTER CHORUS PERFORMANCE HANDBOOK: AN ACTING METHOD FOR SINGERS

THE WESTMINSTER CHORUS PERFORMANCE HANDBOOK: AN ACTING METHOD FOR SINGERS

by Micah Sloat, M.A.

Foreword by Justin Miller, Director of the Westminster Chorus

Edited by Lane Aikin, Will Lagos, and Courtenay R. Crouch, M.A.

Alcove Publishing
2019

The Westminster Chorus Performance Handbook: An Acting Method for Singers

Copyright © 2019 by Micah Sloat, M.A.

First printing: 2019

ISBN 978-1-7332053-0-6
Ebook ISBN 978-1-7332053-2-0

Alcove Publishing

ACKNOWLEDGEMENTS

The Westminster Chorus would like to thank all who have supported us over the years, especially our families, friends, and the fans from all over the world who have been so kind and generous.

We would not be where we are today without the help of the many talented musicians and choreographers who have worked with us. A special thanks to Mark Hale for his early inspiration and support—we would not be here without his encouragement. Continued thanks to Aaron Dale, David Wright, Dr. Greg Lyne, Brett Littlefield, Dawn Castiglione, David McEachern, Erin Howden, and Tony DeRosa. Additionally, our sincerest gratitude to our early musical leadership of Terry Ghiseli and Royce Ferguson whose time and effort can never be fully repaid.

Lastly, we would like to extend a special thanks to those who have been extraordinarily generous in their support of the chorus: John and Sharon Miller, Jackie Palmquist, and Gene Clements.

i

FOREWORD

Music, and especially vocal music, is perhaps the highest form of communication. The combination of poetically and eloquently written text with soul stirring musical composition can elevate the spirit like few other phenomena have the ability to do. However, it takes thought, effort, and quite a bit of work for the music to jump off the printed page and come alive; it is not something that just magically happens.

In my experience, the best work that one can do to elevate choral music even further is work from the heart. Yes, there may be heavy amounts of technical vocal work that is necessary for voices to be in tune, words to be articulate, and for chords to be balanced, but none of that means anything without the work of the heart. In fact, I have witnessed many rehearsals where the specific vocal technique has slowed the pace of the rehearsal to a crawl, but once the conductor allows the singers to use their skills through the lens of the heart instead of the lens of the mind, the vast majority of vocal problems were no longer evident. As humans, the mind can get in our way, but the heart has a way of uniting the senses to bring higher quality art to the forefront.

In the pages to follow, you will learn about a variety of methods to synthesize the technical with the artistic; the mind with the heart. Only then, when the heart is fully open, will the members of the choral ensemble be connected enough to the music and to each other to reach the highest levels of choral art. Only then will members of the audience be able to sit back and allow their spirit to be taken someplace else. Only then can the two parties together, performer and audience, create something that will never be forgotten.

Justin Miller
Director of the Westminster Chorus

PREFACE

The Barbershop Harmony Society (BHS) hosts a singing competition each year, and barbershop singers from all over the world compete for the gold medal and the title of International Champion. Historically, barbershop performances were heavily stylized, with forced smiles, over-the-top emotions, and exaggerated movements. These elements were heavily presentational, in that the performers were showing—as boldly as possible—what they were feeling and doing. The *Presentation* judging category reflected this approach.

Recently, choruses like the Westminster Chorus from Orange County, California, have begun to approach barbershop performance from a different place. This new approach, inspired by musical theater and other acting forms, is grounded in truth. Gone are the forced smiles and exaggerated expressions, in favor of authentic emotions and honest experiences. This new approach has been very successful in a relatively short period of time—so successful, in fact, that the judging category of *Presentation* has been changed to *Performance*. This change represents a seismic shift in the barbershop landscape.

In any paradigmatic shift, there are many who seek a map to the new paradigm. This method is such a map. Here, we present a comprehensive performance method for barbershop singing that (a) is based in truth; (b) cultivates authenticity; and (c) produces spontaneous, living, evolving performances that are exciting and different every time they are performed. This method is designed for singers with little to no acting training, and every technique is grounded in simple, easy-to-access experiences that we all have on a regular basis.

This method was developed for the Westminster Chorus in order to get new members up to speed as fast as possible. We are proud to share it now with the rest of our brothers and sisters, in the BHS and beyond.

CONTENTS

INTRODUCTION

The method presented here is not based on acting tricks or techniques that must be learned, but is rather based on primary experiences, which are fundamental elements of experience that cannot be stripped away, eliminated, or reduced. This method is designed to simply bring awareness to the capacities you already have, so that you can immediately wield them consciously in a performance context.

Although training does help deepen their efficacy, a novice can use these tools with no training at all. This process is not like learning an instrument, whereby you are acquiring a new skill you didn't possess before. It is more like learning how to do breathing exercises. When working with the breath, the first step is to realize that you are already breathing; bringing conscious attention to your breath immediately opens the door to all kinds of powerful practices.

To begin, we discuss the basic framework of the method, which involves learning how to identify the experiences of being in the heart or being in the mind, and how to successfully navigate between them. Since we spend a great deal of our time in rehearsal, we go into detail about how to best utilize this framework in a rehearsal context.

From there, the *keys to performance* are laid out, which are five aspects of primary experience that we can consciously work with to improve a performance. It can be somewhat abstract and overwhelming for the beginner to work with a whole key in its entirety, so each key is separated into three components that can be practiced in a concrete way.

The best way to use this book is to read it in its entirety, then print out the Performance Outline in Appendix A and use it as a reference during rehearsal. At a Westminster Chorus rehearsal, we have it on a large poster board, next to a similar poster for singing technique. You will often hear phrases from the outline, such as "say *yes!*", and "find your *why*" used during rehearsals. Performance is not an intellectual process; it is an experiential one, so this method is designed to be used as a quick reference, to minimize the amount of rehearsal time that is spent giving notes, and to maximize the time spent singing and performing.

THE MIND & THE HEART

> *God guard me from those*
> *thoughts men think*
> *In the mind alone,*
> *He that sings a lasting song*
> *Thinks in a marrow bone . . .*

William B. Yeats

The goal of performance, and thus the primary aim of this method, is for the performer to *live truthfully in the world of the story*. Living truthfully is to act honestly from an authentic impulse. To be in the world of the story is to be present to the circumstances of the story, while allowing the character's identity to live in your body. The state-of-being in which all of these processes are happening freely and organically can be described as living in the *heart*.

The primary obstacles to this process include: fear, judgment, lack of emotional availability, resistance, trying to stay safe, trying to be good, trying to please, trying to do it right, and so on. These problems arise when one tries to approach performance—a heart-based activity—from the mind. The mind wants results, and it tries to engineer these results by controlling the variables in play. (A perfectly logical thing to do.) Mind wants to execute the plan perfectly, to have the right emotion, at the right dynamic, at the right time to make the audience react the right way. Unfortunately, these attempts at control are the very thing that strangles the life out of the performance and separates the performer from the spontaneity and unpredictability that arises naturally from the heart space.

A similar, but opposite, issue arises when we approach mind-based activities from the heart. A logic puzzle doesn't care that you had a bad day; your feelings are utterly irrelevant. If you try to solve the puzzle by having an anxiety attack, you're just going to hurt yourself and accomplish absolutely nothing. It's just as absurd to try to create an emotionally resonant artistic performance with the mind.

So, the aim of this performance method can be restated as *learning how to leave the mind and enter the heart.* As the great acting teacher Sanford Meisner put it, "all good acting comes from the heart, as it were, and there's no mentality in it" (Meisner & Longwell, 1987, p. 37). This movement from mind to heart is the basic framework for our performance method, and as such we will go into some detail about the differences between the two experiences and how they work together, specifically in the context of rehearsal.

MIND

Mind analyzes; it divides things into discrete bits, and then finds patterns in those bits. It creates maps and seeks to understand why things are the way they are, and it seeks out ways to improve whatever it encounters. It judges right and wrong, good and bad, correct and incorrect. Mind uses rational thinking as a means to process, using logic to determine whether or not to reject or accept something based on a given set of axioms. It has a dissociative quality, watching what is happening from a witness place; it is an impartial observer that is tracking, assessing, analyzing, and coming to conclusions about how to proceed based on available evidence.

To get a sense of the world of mind, think about a computer program. It runs on pure logic. There are no emotions involved. If you want a computer to emote, you can program it to simulate emotions, but they will not be actual emotions. This is what happens trying to perform

4

from the mind—it's at best a simulation of emotional truth, and no matter how accurate that simulation is, it will never be the real thing.

HEART

Heart synthesizes; it combines discrete things into a greater whole, creating entirely new things that did not exist before. Heart perceives the truth of what is and is present to things the way they are. Heart accepts whatever it encounters—it may or may not like what it encounters, but either way it accepts that the encountered thing exists. Heart uses emotion to respond spontaneously to the world; emotional responses are the language of the heart, and it uses this language to express values: things that are valued feel good, things that are detested feel bad. Heart has the quality of association; it directly experiences what is happening in an immediate way. Heart is arational.

To sense the world of heart, remember an experience when you were overcome with emotion, such as love, joy, or sadness. There's an immediate quality to the experience—whatever your emotions are, they are happening now, not in the past or the future. This immediate quality puts you "in the room", present and alive. Emotions are unpredictable and spontaneous—you never know exactly what you're going to feel, even if you are doing something you've done many times before. It's this present, spontaneous quality that breathes life into a performance.

THE HIEROGAMY OF HEART & MIND

Once you have identified the heart and mind experiences in yourself, you can start to cultivate an awareness of when one experience is dominant. As complementary opposites, a person can be in one or the other at a given time, but it is very difficult to be in both simultaneously. Indeed, even if it were possible to be consistently split equally between the two, it would be an undesirable state-of-being because each would receive only a fraction of your attention and energy. It is, however, possible to switch rapidly back-and-forth between them. This is a far better approach, as you are able to apply 100% of your energy and attention to the needs of the moment, whether they be analytical or artistic.

Indeed, performance can be seen as an ongoing dance between heart and mind. Mind is essential for structure, consistency, and technical precision. A performance without mind is pure improvisation. Mind decides that there will be fixed notes, rhythms, and lyrics that stay the same between performances. It has specific ideas about how to sing correctly and incorrectly, and about how the emotional plan will develop over the course of the song to deliver the intended effect on the audience. Mind shapes the boundaries of the performance. Those boundaries are like a cup. The director is the sculptor of the cup; he shapes and guides the performance using the mind. Therefore, it's the director's job to hold the mind energy for the chorus.

Heart is like the water that fills the cup. It is the present, emotional energy that breathes life into the notes, rhythms, lyrics, and emotional plan. A performance without heart is, at best, a technical exhibition. It's the performer's job to provide the heart energy, and to that end, the *keys to performance* are tools to help get you out of the mind and into the heart. As a performer, trust that the director is holding the mind energy and he will let you know if there is a need to go into the mind to fix something technical. Don't try to do the director's job for him; do your job, which is to live in the story and fully invest in the truth of the moment.

So, this performance model is a heart-based approach, but remember: the goal is not to eliminate the mind and only be in heart. Both energies, heart and mind, are vitally important processes in life, and in artistic performance. The goal is to have the flexibility to move

6

smoothly back-and-forth between these two states at will, and to be able to identify which state-of-being is most useful at a given time. By developing these skills, and by gaining mastery of how and when to apply them, you can effortlessly switch to the state-of-being needed in a given moment.

REHEARSAL

There are two types of rehearsal: *technical rehearsal* and *artistic rehearsal*, corresponding to whether or not the performer is working primarily in the mind (technical) or the heart (artistic). As stated above, moving back and forth between the two, and knowing how to work with both, are vitally important to successful rehearsal.

TECHNICAL REHEARSAL

Technical rehearsal is the process of putting the plan into the body, so it will come out spontaneously during performance. This requires first creating, and then practicing, a set of *technical circumstances*. In a barbershop setting the technical circumstances include but are not limited to: (a) notes, (b) rhythms, (c) words, (d) dynamics, (e) diction, (f) choreography, and (g) directorial notes.

These circumstances are put into the body through repetition. This repetition builds up muscle memory, which allows you to eventually be able to repeat those actions without conscious thought. This frees up your energy, so you do not need to think about technical details during your performance. Instead, your energy can be used for creative purposes, such as creating and engaging with images and other forms of inspiration. When the circumstances are practiced to the point that they are automatic, the singer is *unconsciously competent* with the given material.

Unconscious competence must be achieved with the technical circumstances before artistic rehearsal can begin. Stopping at *conscious competence*—where you can execute the technical with precision only by using conscious thought—you will be forced to use your mind to remember what you are supposed to do. You will be managing and controlling your performance, using your mind to prevent mistakes instead of investing in the story and the truth of the moment. That is not a performance; it is having a technical rehearsal in front of a live audience.

As such, it is essential that every singer drill the technical circumstances until the point of unconscious competence. If not, keep practicing. Period. There are no exceptions or ways around this. Likewise, the director's job is to provide enough time to allow the singers to fully digest what's expected of them. Last minute choreography changes, for example, can be devastating to a performance, as the singers struggle to remember the technical details instead of living in the story.

One of the most effective ways to run technical rehearsal is with *distributed practice*: 1) practice short sections of music with exacting specificity and many repetitions instead of running larger sections with less detail and fewer repetitions; 2) when working at home, aim for shorter practice sessions more frequently instead of longer sessions once in a while. When rehearsing shorter sections with precision, the mind can really grab on to the details of what's expected, and then diligently work to put those details into the body. With larger sections, a good deal of mind energy is spent moving from place to place, identifying areas that need work but not addressing them adequately before moving on.

During a technical rehearsal, both the singers and the director are in the mind, using their capacity for judgment to ensure that the plan is being practiced accurately. The body learns slowly, but once learned it does not easily forget. Therefore, it's important to practice with precision. Do not casually blow past a wrong note and tell yourself you'll fix it later. Rehearsing something incorrectly without fixing it is the equivalent of building up a bad habit. It's much harder to fix a bad habit than to learn the technical circumstances correctly the first time; give yourself the gift of deliberate, accurate, quality practice.

ARTISTIC REHEARSAL

The goal of performance is to live in the story as the character, having a truthful experience, where images, thoughts, emotions, and memories are spontaneously coming to you without any effort or planning. *The work of artistic rehearsal is to use artistic choice to continually increase specificity as you explore the world of the story.*

Artistic choice is a decision made about the story that increases the specificity of your experiences and brings the world of the story closer to you. Artistic choices can address questions raised by the text, such as: "Who am I singing to? Where am I? What happened in the past that informs this moment?" If you know what your lover looks like, it's a lot easier to talk to them! Effective artistic choices are choices that inspire you, that ignite your imagination. If a choice is evocative, if it takes you on a journey into the world of the story, then continue to work with it. If a choice doesn't have this effect, then make a different choice.

Unlike technical rehearsal, there is no correct or incorrect way to make an artistic choice. Artistic rehearsal uses *aesthetic judgment*, which means that these decisions are a matter of artistic preference, not right and wrong. There are no boundaries to artistic choice. It doesn't have to make sense, and it doesn't have to have meaning to anyone else but you. Aesthetic judgment is *arational* (not governed by logic or reason) and intuitive. To directly experience aesthetic judgment, try to answer a bizarre, nonsensical question like "what is the smell of the color nine?"

For the director, artistic rehearsal is an opportunity to see where the chorus is at, to experiment with new ideas, and to be inspired by what the chorus is bringing forward. The director can use artistic rehearsal to unify the individual expressions of the chorus members by making an artistic choice for the ensemble, such as: (a) an image, (b) a point-of-view, (c) the environment, (d) a relationship, (e) a quality, (f) a character choice, or (g) an intention. If the director suggests that all members of the chorus imagine the same image, for example, the performance will begin to unify itself naturally, without resorting to artifice or emotional choreography.

In life, specificity of circumstances is presented to us without our active effort. For example, every person we meet already has a backstory, ready for us to discover. In performance, the specificity comes from the artistic choices of the performer, combined with the artistic choices of the director, and the given circumstances presented by the text. These three elements determine the set of *artistic circumstances* for a given piece.

As in technical rehearsal, the goal is to become unconsciously competent with the set of artistic circumstances. In artistic rehearsal, you are unconsciously competent when the artistic circumstances visit you spontaneously and without effort. For example, you don't have to summon the image of your lover, they just appear; you don't have to try to put yourself in the world of the story, you're simply there; you don't have to guess what your character wants, you are already having his thoughts.

Unlike technical rehearsal, it is not necessary (or even desirable) to drill artistic circumstances over and over in a rote manner. That can actually dull your emotional responses to the material. The goal is to allow each performance to be alive and unique; trying to achieve the exact same thing every time takes you away from spontaneity and moves you towards predictability. Instead, your work is to increase your commitment to the world of the story by continually increasing the specificity of your artistic choices. Continue to add detail and nuance, to the point where the world of the story is vibrant, alive, and accessible to you; it should be even more colorful and inspiring than your day-to-day physical reality.

Notice that as you explore new discoveries and play with new artistic choices, the ones you've already found will come and join you in a natural, organic way without any conscious effort. In this way, as you increase the detail of your performance, you are rehearsing the artistic choices you've already made.

A few notes regarding the use of artistic choice: trying to make the "right choice" so that you can get a favorable reaction from the audience, or the director, is a trap laid by the mind. There is no "right" choice. The same choice can have totally different effects every time you perform. Let go of trying to be "right", and simply play with whatever you discover in the moment during that particular performance.

Don't "hold on" to an artistic choice. You don't need to force yourself to see an image at a specific point in the song, for example. Once you've made the choice, your work is done. Just be in the moment and let it visit you if it wants to. If it doesn't, maybe make a different choice, but don't force it.

Often the director will make an artistic choice to unify the chorus and to lead the ensemble in a specific direction. It's your job to know if a particular artistic choice works for you personally. If the director's suggestion doesn't work for you, then make a different choice that achieves the director's goal while also working for you as an individual.

Sometimes directors or coaches coming from a different performance paradigm will give result-oriented direction, such as "you need to be more angry". It's your job as a performer to translate the result into artistic choices that will deliver the result. For instance, you could give yourself an image that really pisses you off. Don't fall into the trap of trying to control your emotions directly; that doesn't work and leads to pretense.

A SAFE ENVIRONMENT

In artistic rehearsal the performer should be in the heart and should allow the director to hold all the mind energy. To do this, the performer needs to trust that his artistic impulses can be expressed freely without restriction. This kind of trust is highly sensitive to shame, so to maintain and increase it, artistic rehearsal must take place in a *safe environment*.

A safe environment, for artistic purposes, means that the natural impulses and expressions of the performer are welcomed without judgment or criticism. This does not mean the director cannot give negative feedback; it means that there are boundaries around how and when negative feedback is delivered. Negative feedback ought to follow one rule: never attack the inner artist. The inner artist is the artistic aspect of self. It plays, it creates, it manifests wonderful things, and it must be respected and honored. If a person takes an artistic risk and it does not fit the plan, then praise the performer for having the courage to take that risk and point out that the plan requires a different approach. Attacking the inner artist with criticism by saying their artistic expression was wrong, bad, or that their artistic choices were not good enough, makes the environment artistically unsafe.

In an artistically unsafe environment, the performer will cease to be vulnerable as they try to protect the inner artist and avoid shame. Without vulnerability, the heart closes, and the creative genius provided by the inner artist—along with the spontaneity, creativity, joy, magic, and wonder—leaves the room. The performer compensates by going into the mind and trying to control the performance in order to deliver a performance that will not trigger shame. This retraction into the mind leads to performances without trust that are controlled, inhibited, predictable, and boring.

This rule only applies to the inner artist that lives in the heart. If the performer is not showing up, not present, not taking artistic risks, is stuck in the mind, is controlling, lazy, or otherwise doing something that is not conducive to a successful rehearsal, then it can be appropriate to give them critical feedback in no uncertain terms. Sometimes a performer needs a swift kick in the pants to get out of the mind and into the heart.

(Also, it should be noted that mind loves constructive criticism, and can handle plenty of it during technical rehearsal, as long as the criticism is fair and accurate. In fact, working effectively at a high level of technical detail is the mind's happy place.)

REHEARSAL FLOW

The two rehearsal processes are complementary. During a technical rehearsal, the energy is in the mind, and the artistic component is unconscious. During an artistic rehearsal, the energy is in the heart, and the technical component is unconscious. Since the goal is unconscious competence in each area, the director can work with this feature intentionally to identify what needs work: technical rehearsal reveals what work is needed artistically, and vice versa.

When navigating rehearsal in this way, the director should avoid criticizing the chorus for a technical failure during artistic rehearsal, or an artistic flaw during technical rehearsal. That approach can turn a rehearsal into a series of perceived failures, as the performers strive to achieve one goal only to be criticized for something entirely different that they weren't paying attention to. From a performer's perspective, that feels unfair and is demoralizing.

If a performer feels like they are expected to do everything perfectly all the time, they may try to split their focus and attend to the artistic and the technical simultaneously. When neither the technical nor the artistic are provided with fully committed attention, performance in both areas is generally distracted and of poor quality. This usually leads to ineffective rehearsals, and in turn, to disappointing performances.

Instead, if the director notices a technical flaw during an artistic run-through, he should explicitly mark a shift in focus and move to technical rehearsal. "That was a great performance, thank you! But that major seventh chord isn't tuning so let's fix that real quick." This will allow the singers to go back into the mind to fix the problem. Likewise, if the director notices an area that needs artistic attention during a technical rehearsal, shift to artistic rehearsal to fix it. "We're having trouble following the dynamic plan, but that issue might fix itself when we connect to the meaning of this phrase. Let's leave the technical stuff alone for a minute and go into performance mode."

Working this way, singers can always be 100% focused and committed to the task at hand, because they are clear about exactly what is expected of them at that moment, and they are not trying to do everything at once. During technical rehearsal, they will be fully focused on excellence of technical execution, and during artistic rehearsal, they can fully enter the heart space without judgment.

Working this way will turn rehearsals into a series of small wins. Each success feels good, leading to the next opportunity to improve. It turns the rehearsal process into a joyful march towards excellence. Everyone is on the same page and working together towards a shared goal, supported and inspired by the director's clear vision and focused guidance.

As the rehearsal process matures, the balance of heart and mind shifts. At first, rehearsals consist of technical rehearsal exclusively. As the technical components are learned, more time can be devoted to artistic rehearsal. This process of moving from the technical to the artistic is aided by imbuing the technical elements with artistic meaning. For example, if your choreography is to reach upwards, you can make an artistic choice that you are praying. Now you don't have to remember the move; your artistic choice has tied the lyric, the music, the movement, and the meaning all together into a singular expression, and all you have to do at that moment is pray.

This process helps the mind release the desire to obsess over technical details while taking you closer to the world of the story. It's also an opportunity for the director to provide a unifying artistic vision for the ensemble. Justin Miller, director of the Westminster Chorus, provides a musical plan with three columns on it: (a) Lyrics, (b) Choreography, and (c) Purpose (see Appendix C). For every phrase, the choreography is specified, as well as an artistic suggestion for what that move might mean. The performer can use distributed practice to go through this process at home until every move is learned and imbued with meaning.

THE KEYS TO PERFORMANCE

The *keys to performance* are five elements of everyday experience that are consciously utilized during artistic rehearsal to transport the performer to the heart space in a reliable way. Like the breath, the keys to performance are naturally occurring capacities of being that we use all the time whether we are aware of it or not. So, we simply need to wield their power by conscious choice. The five keys are: (a) *presence*, (b) *focus*, (c) *will*, (d) *character*, and (e) *trust*.

The keys themselves can seem abstract and complex. Therefore, each key is broken down into three components, or *tools*, that can be practiced in a concrete way. During rehearsal, you can work with the tools exclusively. For example, by working on the components of will (values, intention, and stakes) you are doing the work necessary to activate the will; you don't need to try to work on "will" itself.

Each tool is accompanied by a phrase summarizing the essence of the tool. You can use these casual terms as a mnemonic aid, for example, instead of remembering the academic terms "object, action, environment," you can simply remember "who, what, where". The academic terms exist so that the method can be laid out formally and accurately; the casual terms are for quick, practical use in a rehearsal setting. A working reference for both can be found in Appendix A.

PRESENCE

Presence is the state-of-being in which you are perceiving what is happening in the present moment and reacting to it spontaneously. Presence is a defining quality of heart-based experiences; if you are in the heart, you are present. Likewise, if you are not in the heart, being present will take you there. Therefore, presence is a primary tool to find and enter the heart space.

All the other keys to performance require and assume a baseline level of presence. Without presence, you can have a highly developed character, a very clear intention, a precise action, and an effortless trust in your impulses, but these assets might not enter the room and affect the audience. Presence puts you in the room, creating a bridge that connects you to the audience via empathy.

Empathy is the capacity to experience what another person is going through. Mirror neurons in the brain can automatically bring us into experiential attunement with someone else (Winerman, 2005); this is how the performing arts can take us on a journey. In a movie, for example, we sync up with characters on the screen as we share thoughts and feelings empathically. In a moving piece of music, the emotions of the performer affect how they sing; effectively, the emotions are encoded into sound waves. The sound waves travel through the air, and we reconstitute those emotions in our own being.

Without presence, one side of the connection is not there. The performer may be having profound experiences, but they need to be shared with the audience in order to affect them. Watching a performance is like watching a dream. A performer that is asleep may be having very intense and meaningful visions, but until he wakes up and embodies those visions—until they allow all their internal experiences to be expressed—the dream will remain hidden from the audience.

Presence is experiential; it's something you can practice. To practice presence, we can actively work on the three primary components of presence: (a) *discovery*, (b) *acceptance*, and (c) *vulnerability*.

DISCOVERY
WHAT'S NEW IN THIS MOMENT?

Discovery is the process of realizing what is new and different in every moment. Allow yourself to be surprised

20

by what you find as you stand at the crossroads of time between the past and the future. You are an active participant in the unfolding of history. The universe itself is alive, changing and moving in an eternal cosmic dance. What can you discover right now? You may have sung this song before, but every run-through is unique. What is different this time? What surprises wait for you in the next phrase? Michael Chekov, the great Russian actor, was a master of discovery. Those who watched his performances felt that "every night his performance had a totally different feeling to it. His stage actions were improvised nightly" (Chekov, 1991, p. xx.).

The opposite of discovery is preconception. If you have a preconceived idea about how the performance should go, and you stick to that plan at all costs, regardless of what is really happening in the moment, then your performance will tend to be predictable, boring, and uninspired. Why?

You cannot fool empathy. If you try to show the audience that you are happy when you are really not, the audience will not perceive someone that is happy. They will see someone who is not happy and is trying hard to cover it up by imitating happiness. If you know what is going to happen next, then the audience is watching someone who knows what will happen next. This is predictable, safe, and boring. There is nothing new to provide anticipation or surprise when you have already decided exactly what will happen during your performance; that's the equivalent of turning yourself into a performing robot.

The audience wants to see something that feels alive, that feels real. They want to feel like anything could happen at any moment. Since you cannot fool the audience, you have to actually have an experience yourself that is alive and real. If you are using discovery, then you really, truly do not know what is going to happen next; you do not know how it is going to happen, and you are ready at any moment for something new and crazy to take place, just like an exciting situation in any other context. "When we drop the blinders of our preconceptions, we are virtually propelled by every circumstance into the present time and the present mind: the moment, the whole moment, and nothing but the moment" (Nachmanovitch, 1990, p. 22).

When you release control and start to discover what is actually happening in each moment, you may be saying words you have said before, but you do not know how you are going to say them. You might know the artistic circumstances of the piece, but not know which emotions you are going to feel about them today. The more you release control, the more you are able to experience how this moment is unlike any moment that has come before, and any moment that will ever come after. This is the glory of the present!

ACCEPTANCE
SAY "YES" TO EVERYTHING.

Acceptance means saying "yes" to whatever is happening in the moment. When you make a discovery, you can react to it by accepting and acknowledging what you discovered, or you can deny its existence and continue on as if you did not notice it at all. Saying "yes" brings you closer to presence because it connects you to the unfolding of the moment and makes you a participant instead of an observer. To practice acceptance, simply take the attitude that everything that is happening is right. "Yes! This is what is happening, and I'm going with it."

Accept that whatever you are experiencing is right and appropriate for the character in that situation at that moment. If necessary, integrate the experience by justifying it: allow the discovery to have a background that informs the character's experience in that moment. For example, if you are sad when the performance plan calls for joyful singing to your beloved, perhaps there is a part of you that is secretly sad you will have to leave her soon. Integrating complex discoveries like this are not only okay, they can spark moments of artistic genius.

In contrast, saying no, or denying what is happening in the moment, puts you into the mind and into the witness position. Instead of actively engaging in the moment, denial separates you and disconnects you from what is happening around you. Having a preconceived notion of how the show is supposed to go, and then holding fast to that idea, sets you up to make mistakes, which are only possible if you apply judgment to your performance.

If there is a discovery that does not fit with the musical plan or the choreography, that is okay. You must discover and accept what is happening because what is happening is the truth. If your voice cracks or part of the set falls down, you will be a lot better off if you choose to acknowledge and work with those facts in an artistic way than if you ignore them as if it did not happen.

VULNERABILITY

STAY OPEN AND SEEN.

To be vulnerable is to have the courage to be affected, and to be seen. To be affected means to remove the protection around your heart so that the circumstances of the story can generate *authentic impulses.* Authentic impulses are truthful, spontaneous reactions to stimuli. These impulses can inspire physical movement, emotions, thoughts, visions, and anything else you're capable of. When you are open in this way, these impulses provide a constant stream of living inspiration that makes every moment unique.

Amazing discoveries, and interesting, spontaneous reactions are only interesting to the audience if they can share the experience with you. When you allow yourself to be seen, you are sharing your truth with them. When they can see your real thoughts and your emotions, you begin to connect to the audience through empathy. When the empathic connection is made, they start to go on the journey with you. Without empathy, at best they are hearing pleasing sounds and watching a technically accurate performance. Empathy is necessary for the performance to matter.

True vulnerability in front of an audience can be scary for new performers. (True vulnerability can be scary in most contexts.) You're exposing your authentic impulses. You might feel naked. You might feel exposed. Yet, this is the place where the performer must live. To show up in this place consistently is to have *artistic courage*. The more you expose yourself, the more interesting you become. As the audience forges an empathic connection with you, they enter the heart with you. Judgment is a mind-based activity, so paradoxically, the more vulnerable you are, the less likely they are to judge you. Show your truth without hiding. "If you expose your limitations and let people see them, you no longer have anything to hide" (Morris & Hotchkis, 2002, p. 15).

FOCUS

Focus is about directing our awareness so we can be present to what is most important. Presence brings us into connection with what is happening, but not all things happening have equal weight. By focusing our attention, we can hold our awareness towards a specific object. Since we are often communicating with someone else on stage, the object of our focus is frequently another character in the story. Presence is spontaneous, and it follows natural impulse without control. When we hold focus, it allows us to create a narrower playing field for presence to play inside of, so we can simultaneously be free and present, while paying attention to what matters the most.

> There is no good acting without intense focus and concentration. Even the character who is supposedly relaxed and casual has something on which his life or lifestyle at the moment is centered. Find it, focus on it, concentrate. (Barr, 1997, p. 33)

Focus also directs the energy of the will. Energy without direction is like a firehose without anyone holding it: it has a lot of power, but it will be dispersed over a wide area and it will be random in its application. Focus allows us to grab a hold of the metaphorical hose and aim it at something of value.

The three primary components of focus are: (a) *object*, (b) *action*, and (c) *environment*, often referred to as *who*, *what*, *where*. The object of your attention is often, but not necessarily, another character in the story; you need to know who you are talking to. You must take a specific action in relation to the object of our focus. Watching someone do nothing isn't very interesting, so as the story unfolds, at any given moment you should know exactly what you are doing. We also want to be aware of the context—we want to know about where we are taking action because situational awareness affects how an action is executed. "Convincing a friend to believe you" in a library is much different from taking that same action at a rock concert. Awareness of the surrounding environment also provides important resources for inspiration, often in the form of sensations, such as what sights, sounds, and other experiences are waiting for you.

OBJECT
WHO AM I TALKING TO?

At any given moment in the piece, you must be able to precisely identify the object of your focus. Object types can be categorized by the position you take in relationship to them. You can take the first-person position, focusing on yourself. This includes anytime you are having an internal conversation, such as in a monologue or a soliloquy. The second person position is focusing on someone else, such as another character in the story, either imaginary or as embodied by another performer. The third person position is focusing on a thing, such as the sunrise. There is a fourth position, which in performance is also referred to as *breaking the fourth wall*, where the object of your focus is the audience. You can also use the fourth position to talk to God, or to the universe itself.

No matter who or what you are focusing on, it must be specific and real to you. If you are talking to another character, you must know who you are talking to. What does she look like? What is her point-of-view? What does she want? What is your relationship to her? What does she believe in? What else is important to know about this character? In order to answer these questions, first look to the text to see if the answers are in the story. If not, use your imagination and intuition to make artistic choices. Dig deep to find specific and interesting details about the character so that you are inspired to communicate.

ACTION
WHAT AM I DOING TO THEM?

An action is a verb that describes what you are literally doing to the object of your focus. What are you doing? Are you fighting, cajoling, pushing, begging, or pleading? This is not complicated; it is simply a literal description of what it is you are doing in the story. Later, we will add intention, which is what you want to accomplish by doing this action. The tension between what you are doing and what you want generates interesting layers of complexity.

Every action has a *goal*, or a target that will determine whether or not the action was successful. What is the goal? How will you know if your action succeeded or failed? This will later interact with the will, feeding into your stakes.

Every action has a *quality*. This is a fun place to play around and experiment. How are you pursuing your action? For example, if your action is convincing, and your object is your mother, are you doing it softly, aggressively, or slyly? What way feels the best? What new ways can you discover? There is a lot of room here to play. In rehearsal, try experimenting with qualities as a way of finding new ways to approach the material.

26

Look for a way of describing your action that inspires you and gets you excited to do it. You can add adjectives to color it and make it fun. You can even add imaginary images, or you could describe it in a totally crazy way. For example, you could change "I'm convincing my mother to let me take the car tonight" into "I've got to con the jailer into give me the keys so I can bust out of this prison!" This is not an intellectual exercise. It is about fueling your spirit and animating your body by stoking the fires of passion.

ENVIRONMENT
WHERE AM I?

The environment is the landscape in which the story is taking place. Where are you? Some songs are specific about the environments they require. If there are no specific textual requirements, and if the director has not specified an environment, then you have the option to build your environment with as much or as little detail as serves your artistic spirit. Either way, let your imagination play freely. What does the song do to you? Do you see a lake, a mountain, a magical landscape? Does your beloved laugh in a field? Does she sit by the water? Allow yourself to live in the world of the song.

> During every moment we are on the stage, during every moment of the development of the action of the play, we must be aware either of the external circumstances which surround us (the whole material setting of the production), or of an inner chain of circumstances which we ourselves have imagined in order to illustrate our parts. (Stanislavski, 1989, p. 63)

All characters and objects in the story also have a *location*. This is the physical place in the performance space that they appear. You must know where the object of your focus is located in the space, because if you do not know where it is, the audience certainly will not. This is especially important if the entire chorus is focusing on the same object.

WILL

Will is the physical energy that pursues desire. It lives in the body and it animates you to move in pursuit of what you want. Will can be understood as the active position you choose to take in relationship to the circumstances. Will is what makes your point-of-view active and animated. It drives your action and gives fuel to everything you do on stage.

Will lives in the body, just like emotions do, but it is different from emotions in that your emotions are spontaneous reactions to circumstances that come and go, while will is constant and drives you towards what you desire. If you are pursuing a lover, you may experience joy or sadness along the way; the will to be united with your lover is underneath both of those emotions, constant, driving you through all kinds of experiences, leading you as you pursue your mission.

On stage, your will must always be actively in pursuit of something. Watching someone with no will is boring. Even if the events of the story lead to being unable to fulfill your desire, or if your character has a breakdown or a moment of tragedy, there is always a different kind of drive on the other side. If a lover loses his love, his intention may change from love to revenge. Or he may even have the will to die. No matter what happens, the will must always be actively engaged in pursuit of something that matters. This drives the narrative and provides the story with vitality. As Hollywood acting coach Tony Barr (1997) put it, "energy is the direct result of how much you care about what is happening" (p. 37).

To clearly define what drives your character's will in the story, we need to look at (a) *values*, (b) *intention*, and (c) *stakes*. Values are the beliefs that determine what your character cares about. Intention is the active pursuit of realizing those values in the world of the story. Stakes determine what your character has to gain, and what he is at risk of losing.

VALUES
WHY AM I DOING THIS?

Values determine what you want. There are many kinds of values. Moral values are concerned with right and wrong. Personal preferences are values that determine what you love and what you hate. Needs are values based on practical concerns, such as survival, so they are ultimately about what is useful or useless in a given circumstance. Judgments are value-based decisions about what you consider to be bad or good given a set of criteria. What all of these have in common is that they are a fundamental component of identity. What a character wants (or doesn't want) is essential in differentiating that character from the other characters in the story.

A character's set of values is his or her *beliefs*, and these beliefs interact with the circumstances, creating a *point-of-view*. Point-of-view can also be understood as specificity of perspective. A character that values power, for example, will have a different point-of-view on warfare than a character who values peace. Conflict between sets of values—either inside of a single character or between characters—is one of the most important ways of generating interesting dramatic situations.

To discover a character's values, first go to the text. What is in the text that requires a specific point-of-view? What value establishes that point of view? For example, if your character is singing a love song, then you might state his point-of-view as *my lover is everything*. The value that drives that point-of-view could be "love is the most important thing in the world." You can state a point-of-view and a value anyway you like; your job is to find a way of phrasing it that heightens your emotions and ignites the will to action. Repeat this as necessary so you have a strong and clear point-of-view for every moment in the text.

To add layers of interest to your performance, you may choose to discover additional values your character may hold that are not immediately derived from the text. The more you know about what your character values, the more complex and nuanced your performances can be. For example, in a love song, your character's moral values may not be specifically referenced in the text. But perhaps your character cares deeply about doing the right thing, and the love of his life has been tricked into spending time with another man who is trying to take her down a dark path. Now your character is not just expressing his love—he is saving her life and fighting for moral justice. In a case like this, the audience might have no awareness of these private discoveries, but you have provided yourself an additional layer of interesting complexity that can inform your performance.

INTENTION
WHAT DO I WANT?

Intention is the clear and specific pursuit of desire. Intention describes how you are going to get what you want. Values determine what you want, intention is your active mission to obtain it. Intention combines action and desire; it is action in pursuit of desire. Action is what you are doing. Intention is the reason you are doing it. Having a strong intention is a bedrock, cornerstone principle for performance. As the great acting teacher Constantin Stanislavski (1989) wrote, "On the stage, do not run for the sake of running, or suffer for the sake of suffering. Don't act 'in general', for the sake of action; always act with a purpose" (p. 40).

Another way of understanding intention is as vision. What vision does your character hold that he is aiming at? What is the target of his desire? What does that picture look like? If you hold the picture of what you want in your mind, and you pursue the realization of that image, you are acting with intention. Note that the vision must be pursued. A vision without action attached to it is a plan, not an intention.

Your job is to find an intention that inspires you, that enlivens the emotions, that makes you so fired up that you pursue it with relentless passion. To do this, discover and state what your intention is. If it feels academic or theoretical, or if it just does not engage your emotions enough, rephrase the intention. Keep changing the phrasing until you find a way of phrasing it that truly ignites the will to passionate action.

Intention can change when the circumstances of the story change. Identify in the text when these changes occur, if they do at all, and make sure you have a clear intention for each section.

STAKES
WHAT HAPPENS IF I SUCCEED/FAIL?

Stakes describe what happens if you succeed and what happens if you fail. Will is like an engine, and it must have fuel. The fuel of the will is the *stakes*. Make the stakes vivid and real by imagining them in detail. If you succeed, what happens? If your lover agrees to spend her life with you, what will that look like? If you defeat the enemy, what happens next? In life, we are constantly envisioning possible futures that we desire. An actor gives Oscar acceptance speeches in the shower; a child who wants to be a doctor performs surgery on dolls; a person in love has fantasy after fantasy of being with the object of their affections. Each time this is done, the intention is clarified and the commitment to success is renewed.

Likewise, fear is also a powerful motivator. What happens if you fail? What if your lover rejects you? What if you cannot defeat the enemy? These are unpleasant thoughts. In life, these kinds of thoughts can chase a person like a hungry wolf. Often, these thoughts are pushed out of conscious awareness, but when action is required to avoid such a path, a person will do whatever it takes to avoid it, as long as doing so is congruent with their values—and sometimes even if it is not. Your character may not need to dwell on these negative

31

thoughts, but he should know exactly what horrors lie in store for him if he does not succeed in his mission.

Your stakes must be deep and important to you; you must have high stakes. Stakes are not cookie-cutter, and they are not intellectual. You must find stakes that evoke strong reactions from you emotionally. If you think of your stakes and you do not feel driven to succeed, and if you are not determined with all your being to accomplish your task, then your stakes are not high enough.

CHARACTER

Character is the difference between the who you are in life, and who you are onstage. Every song requires a specific point-of-view, it requires you to have a personal relationship to the material, and it requires you to know what you are singing about. These elements are referred to in this performance model as (a) *identity*, (b) *relationship*, and (c) *history*, and together they help develop character.

Each element of character can be approached from two directions. The first approach is to use historical events from our own past that are similar in nature to access the character's reality. This is called *personalization*. To use this tool, think of a memory that has similar emotional content as the piece you are working with. The emotions associated with the memory will arise in your body. While these emotions are living in you, switch your point-of-view to your character, and live in the circumstances of the story. For example, if your character is experiencing sadness and loss due to the loss of a loved one, you could think of a time when you yourself felt deep sadness and loss, perhaps the time when you lost someone close to you. When you start feeling those emotions, let go of the memory, and instead think about the loss your character is experiencing. How was the emotion caused by the events in the story? Live through these events. Get specific about them. Experiencing the old emotions and the new circumstances together at the same time wires the two together in your brain, so when you think about the character's situation, those emotions of loss will be triggered at the same time.

When using personalization, we are intentionally accessing memories that have emotional importance to our default identity. Therefore, there may be a natural tendency to want to enter the memory—to re-experience it, to process it, to explore it, or otherwise stay with it for a while. These memories, however, are not the character's memories, and beyond their similar emotional content, they may not be relevant to what is happening in the story. If you dwell on them, you may drift away from the circumstances your character is living in. This can lead to having experiences on stage that are not relevant to the text, that do not match the rest of the performance or the other performers, and that generally make you less present as you become wrapped up in personal material the audience has no access to.

Thus, when using personalization, it is very important to take the final step and make sure that you have gone through the process of letting go of the original memory as you attach the emotions to the events your character is living through. Personalization does not mean having personal memories during a performance. It is a rehearsal tool, used to awaken the emotions so that they respond with passion as you are living truthfully through the circumstances of the story.

The second approach to developing character is to use *imagination*. Your character lives in a set of imaginary circumstances. You must know what those circumstances are, they must be specific, and they must be meaningful to you. To use imagination to develop character, first identify everything in the story that your character knows about that is a mystery to you, the performer. These may include anything a person can experience, including (a) memories, (b) events, (c) images, (d) knowledge, (e) relationships, and (f) beliefs. For each item on the list, create that experience for yourself in your imagination. Daydream it. Live through it as vividly as possible. After you do this, you will have that experience encoded in your brain; now you are ready to re-experience that memory during your artistic rehearsals, as you further explore the world of the story.

IDENTITY
WHO AM I?

Identity describes who you are when you are on stage. The difference between you and the character is largely arbitrary. There are simply two identities: the identity of the character, and your default identity that you walk around the world with. In performance, you make the choice to associate with the identity of the character, and you give your default identity a break. You are still you in the sense that your consciousness—the point of awareness in spacetime that is perceiving the world—is the same, but you take on everything else that belongs to your character, such as his name, memories, beliefs, emotions, and thoughts. So, when you are on stage, you are the character. "It was as if Gogol's Khestakov, once given life on stage, began to direct the actor Chekhov" (Chekov, 1991, p. xx).

To build your identity, start with the work you've already done: your values, your beliefs, your intention, and your point-of-view. These form the core of your identity, and they point to *archetype*. An archetype is a universal identity that can appear in an infinite number of contexts. For example, the hero, or the mother, are both identities that have an infinite number of expressions, and they appear all over the place in fiction and in life throughout history. What archetype, or archetypes, describe your character? Are they a villain? A lover? A rebel?

Once you know the basic archetype you're working with, try to get more specific. If you're a hero, what kind of hero are you? A tragic hero? An anti-hero? A reluctant hero? How is the expression of this archetype unique to this particular piece? When you reach this point, you can begin to flesh out your Identity by filling in the details.

Ask yourself *what do I need to know about my character*? You do not need an exhaustive list of everything about your character. Your character's favorite breakfast cereal is most likely irrelevant to performing a love song. You do, however, need to answer all the important questions. Look at the text for: 1) what the text says explicitly about your character, (b) what the text implies about your character, and (c) what your imagination wants to know about your character that is not spelled out in the text. Use artistic choice to answer all unknown or ambiguous questions.

RELATIONSHIP
WHO ARE WE?

Relationship describes your connection to the other characters and the events that occur in the world of the story. Relationships to other characters are just like the relationships we have with others in a non-performance context. In life, the specificity of these relationships is accomplished for us without effort. When performing, we need to generate this specificity.

A good place to start is with *relationship type*. Every relationship to a character has a type. For example, parent-child or teacher-student are two different types of relationships. The balance of power in the relationship is called *status*. Status and type can combine in interesting ways. For example, if you're the student in a teacher-student relationship, you can still have higher status than the teacher. If the type of relationship is romantic, who has the status? Does that change over the course of the performance?

Your relationship to events in the story is also analogous to events in life. When something important happens to us, we have a point-of-view that is determined by our values. We also have a level of *power* that determines our ability to affect the situation. Are you in control, or are you a victim? Are you a participant or an observer? Are you in danger or are you reaping rewards? Get specific about how the event affects you and get specific about your ability to affect the event. When you know where you stand in relationship to the events happening around you, you are ready to act.

HISTORY
HOW DOES THE PAST AFFECT THE PRESENT?

History describes how the past informs the present. Your character has a set of past experiences, and you must use personalization and/or imagination to make those experiences accessible to you. For example, if you are singing to your sweetheart about the good times you have had together, you must know what those good times were! To do this, first identify all the moments in the song that explicitly call for a memory, such as references to past events or circumstances of the song that require backstory. Next, allow your imagination to construct the memory for you. The more vivid it is to you, the better. If you are alone at home, act it out if you can, so you have the experience of living through the memory in the first person. If your emotions are responding to the memory, the work is ready to be worked with in artistic rehearsal. If you are not responding emotionally, use personalization or re-imagine it until it affects you.

After you have all the explicit memories, gather the implicit ones. These are memories that are not directly mentioned in the text of the song, but that you feel would be necessary for your character to have. For example, if you are singing a love song, there may not be any memories specifically mentioned in the song, but you ought to give yourself some memories of being together anyway, for obvious reasons! As a general rule, provide yourself with at least three implicit memories for each major relationship in the piece.

Lastly, give yourself any other memories that you feel would enhance your performance. For example, if there is a piece in Latin, perhaps you want to dream about what it would be like to live as a monk in 12th century

Europe. These images can add color and nuance when they visit you in the song.

This work is about feeding your artistic spirit, it is not about checking off boxes. If you are not actively involved in the process, it will not be meaningful. Do this work from a joyful, inspired place where you are excited to explore your character and the world of the song.

TRUST

Trust is about faith in yourself, and faith in the universe. When you trust yourself, you can show up with what you have, and have that be enough. When you trust the universe, you can take artistic risks and trust that whatever happens will be okay. When you have all the other pieces in place, and when you have done the work during rehearsal necessary to gain unconscious competence with the material, trust is what makes the magic happen. "The depths are obscured in us when we try to force feelings; we clarify them by giving them adequate time and space and letting them come" (Nachmanovitch, 1990, p. 141).

Without trust in the self, the mind can start to intrude and try to control the performance as a way to avoid shame. Without trust in the universe, safety is often chosen over risk. Instead of making discoveries, the performer clings to the plan like a life raft. Both of these approaches lead to controlled, predictable, and inauthentic performances.

Trust may seem like an abstract concept, but we can consciously work on developing trust by working with the components of trust: (a) *truth*, (b) *play*, and (c) *risk*.

TRUTH
THE TRUTH IS ENOUGH.

To tell the truth, you have to trust that the truth, as it is, is enough. If you think that the truth is not enough, and you embellish the truth in an attempt to make it more interesting, it's no longer the truth. You literally can't embellish the truth and tell the truth as it is at the same time. Therefore, the practice of sticking with the truth, as it is, will ground you in presence and authenticity.

By accepting the moment as it arises and saying *this is enough*, you are free to discover and share what you find without shame. You do not have to worry if it is interesting enough, or emotional enough, or whether it is technically correct, or whether the director likes it. Whatever happens is enough. No matter where you are at on a particular day, that is where you are. Whatever emotions come or do not come, however strong or subtle they are, that is exactly right for that moment. Have no concern with how emotional you are being or not being; be fully and completely invested in the story, and let whatever honest emotions come and go as they will. The truth is more interesting and important than any plan, and you have to start with the truth if you want the magic to happen. "Truth on the stage is whatever we can believe in with sincerity, whether in ourselves or in our colleagues. Truth cannot be separated from belief, nor belief from truth. They cannot exist without each other" (Stanislavski, 1936, p. 129).

You can't fool the audience. If, for some reason, you are only feeling mild sadness in a moment that calls for intense tragedy, and you're honest with your expression, the audience might respond with "hmm...that was an interesting way to play that moment. Very understated." If you try to force extreme sadness when it's not real, the audience will likely respond with "that was terrible" or a similar judgment. Far better to have the first reaction. Always stay with the truth. The smallest truth is more interesting than the biggest lie.

If you have a run-through where your level of investment in the story is not where you, or the director, would like it to be, then note that and adjust your artistic choices to make them more intense. Raise the stakes. Make the visions more detailed. Add to your relationship to make it more precarious. Do whatever is necessary to increase your investment in the circumstances, but *do not lie* to yourself or to the audience.

If you get in the habit of faking it, you are robbing yourself of the opportunity to become a fully realized performer. You are also not fooling anyone except yourself. The audience can see your inauthenticity, and they don't like it. Always stay with the truth.

PLAY
WORK WITH JOY AND CREATIVITY.

To play is to approach whatever you are doing with joy and creativity. Ultimately, performance is playing pretend in front of an audience. A child does this instinctively. This childlike freedom is what allows us to go into the world of the story and live in it as the character. To play is to invite the inner artist to use the stage as a canvas, to paint with visions and impulses, to create an entire world and then set out on an adventure inside of it.

Whenever you are performing, or in an artistic rehearsal, play with whatever you have got at that time. No matter how much preparation you did or did not do, no matter how confident you feel, choose to take the attitude that *I have everything I need.* Choose to be in the heart space, be present, discover, to be creative, and to work with joy. Enjoy the freedom of discovery and adventure that is performance. A child can play with a broken toy without knowing or caring that it is broken. You can perform with what you have, even if there is more work to be done.

The opposite is believing that your work is never enough. Since the imagination is infinite, there is always more work you can do to make the world of the story more specific. You can always improve your technical precision. If you only give yourself permission to let go and perform when you've done enough rehearsal, then you are likely to remain in a state of perpetual striving. The performer's desire to be good has nothing to do with the character's journey through the world of the story. So, paradoxically, trying to be good at living in the story

39

can block you from the experience of actually doing it. Developing the habit of play, and assuming that you have everything you need, will dispel the performer's insecurities and will bring the world of the story into the performance space.

Sometimes, performers confuse technique and artistry, as if by gaining more technique, it makes you a better artist. That is not accurate. The technique gives your inner artist more tools to play with, more tricks to use, more colors of paint to work with, but your inner artist has always known how to play and make art. It does not need technique or instruction or schooling or a degree, all it needs is a safe space to play in without being attacked by judgment.

> Music Lessons were not enjoyable to you as a child because you could already play. Your Music teacher forced you to play scales, fingerings, and rudiments, but did not allow you to play freely, and that, you felt, held you back. . . . Even now you feel that way about practicing. You do not want to practice; you just want to play. So if you feel that practice is necessary, it would benefit you to figure out how to practice while you play so that you can make the most of both. (Wooten, 2006, p. 251)

RISK
CHOOSE COURAGE OVER SAFETY.

Artistic risk is about choosing courage over safety. The present moment is inherently unpredictable. If you're truly present, you don't know what's going to happen next. You don't know how you're going to feel. You don't know what images will or will not appear. You don't know how the audience is going to react. There's an invisible threshold to this experience of the present moment, and to cross that threshold is to risk allowing anything and everything to be possible.

40

These unknowns trigger all sorts of resistance. "What if I feel the wrong emotions? What if I feel nothing? What if my impulses make me do something weird? What if the audience doesn't react the way I want? What if I do it WRONG?!" The answer to all these questions is to summon your artistic courage and step across the threshold anyway. Allowing the possibility that anything may happen includes embracing the possibility of all your fears coming true, including embarrassment, pain, shame, and failure. By saying yes to all possible experiences, you open the doors to everything, and that takes courage.

Staying safe, being afraid of mistakes and clinging to what is known, trying to engineer a performance that will work and won't trigger embarrassment or negative judgment—that may work, to some extent. But by limiting the possibility of great failure, you also limit the possibility of great genius. When you keep your performance restricted to a narrow bandwidth of possibilities that you are afraid to deviate from, at best you deliver a decent performance that people view as polished and adequate. At worst, it's boring, lifeless, and tedious for the audience. Staying safe, therefore, precludes you from truly great performances. And since that's precisely what we're aiming for, you must choose courage over safety.

On stage, mistakes have an interesting feature. The audience doesn't know how the performance is supposed to go, so something that may be a "mistake" to you is not a mistake to the audience until you signal it as such. For example, if you trip on stage, and you awkwardly get up, embarrassed, and look around like you did something horribly wrong, then you're clearly telling the audience you did something wrong. If, instead, you trip but stay present, saying "yes" to the experience and using play to spontaneously incorporate your fall as part of the story, you might have an impulse to reach out to a brother close to you on stage. If he is also present and saying "yes", he will help you up and you two can share a heartwarming moment of support and brotherhood. Now, instead of a mistake, you've created a moment of connection that is both totally unexpected and interesting. In this way, mistakes are not something to be feared; they are opportunities for artistic genius.

When you risk by leaping off the edge of the present moment into the unknown, all of a sudden, every moment becomes an opportunity for this kind of play. Inspirational discoveries pop up, visions appear, thoughts you've never had before come to you. Leap, and let the universe catch you. "When one surrenders in the vast emptiness one is perhaps better equipped than ever to be and act in tune with the ways of the universe" (Nachmanovitch, 1990, p. 147).

When you let go of expectations, you will start to receive these unexpected gifts. When you do not know what is going to happen, and yet you stay present and engaged, pursuing your intention, you will be met with discoveries and surprises that are opportunities for artistic genius. This is the difference between a technically correct performance and a work of art. The technician executes the plan. The artist uses the plan as a launchpad.

CONCLUSION

The goal of performance is to live truthfully in the world of the story. To achieve this goal, the technical aspects first must be learned to the point of unconscious competence. Then, you can focus on leaving the mind and entering the heart by using the *keys to performance*— more specifically, the three practical tools that activate each *key*. We've discussed how to use these tools in rehearsal; let's go over how to use these tools at home, so you have a concrete grasp of exactly what to do throughout the artistic process, from first getting the sheet music to the final performance.

Presence is an in-the-moment experience; there is no "homework" associated with it, and you don't need to prepare anything to be present. You can practice presence simply by applying the tools of presence in whatever situation you are in, including contexts not related to performance. For example, when you're on a date, you can practice presence. What can you discover about the other person? What can you accept about them? How can you be vulnerable? You will find that presence brings a living magic of excitement and spontaneity to anything upon which it is brought to bear.

Focus, will, and *character* are where the "homework" lies. Look at the Performance Worksheet in Appendix B. Ask yourself these questions, and then *daydream* the answers. Live through the imaginary experiences. Write them down. If there are any moments in the piece where the who/what/where/why changes, answer the questions again for each new situation. After you have done this process, you have accomplished the minimum this method requires of you. (Which is no small feat. Thank your inner artist, and celebrate!)

To increase the specificity of your artistic choices, you can repeat this process, each time adding more detail to the world of the story. The initial questions proposed are the just the beginning—a catalyst for inspiration. If other questions come to you, answer them, and continue to ask questions about the piece, filling in the world with evocative detail provided by the inner artist as he paints the inner landscape using the imagination.

Focus, will, and *character* are not limited to the world of the story; they are forces in daily life as well. By bringing conscious attention to how these forces operate all around us, we can better understand how they work and how we can use them. Look at the stories people are living in all around you. Notice how their values determine their point-of-view, and shape the actions they take. Notice how someone with a clear intention will drive toward it relentlessly, while someone who doesn't know what they want drifts wherever the tides of life may take them. Watch how a situation with great stakes creates intense drama, and how important events in the past shape what happens today. The forces of *focus, will,* and *character* are operating all around us, all the time.

Trust is like presence in that it is practiced experientially. You can approach every interaction with the basic premise: "my truth is enough". What happens when you aren't concerned with putting on a mask? When you stop selling yourself as bigger or smaller than you really are? When you let go of trying to get a specific reaction out of someone? What happens when you approach the activity in front of you with joy and creativity? Can your busy job be an opportunity for play? What opportunities do you have in life to ignore the voice of fear, to leave the place of emotional safety and take courageous risks?

At this point, it may occur to you that the *keys to performance* are not simply ways to improve your performance, they are broadly applicable tools for being alive. For if performing is to live truthfully in the world of the story, as we learn to perform, so do we learn how to live. For to live truthfully is to possess the power to be truly yourself, and to craft the world of the story is to learn how to craft the story of your own life.

44

APPENDIX A: METHOD OUTLINE

PRESENCE	DISCOVERY	What's *new*?
	ACCEPTANCE	*Say "yes" to all things.*
	VULNERABILITY	Stay *open* and *seen*.
FOCUS	OBJECT	*Who* am I talking to?
	ACTION	*What* am I doing to them?
	ENVIRONMENT	*Where* am I?
WILL	VALUES	*Why* am I doing this?
	INTENTION	What do I *want*?
	STAKES	What if I *succeed / fail*?
CHARACTER	IDENTITY	Who am *I*?
	RELATIONSHIP	Who are *we*?
	HISTORY	What is in the *past*?
TRUST	TRUTH	The *truth is enough.*
	PLAY	Work with *joy* & *creativity.*
	RISK	Choose *courage*.

BE IN THE HEART | LIVE IN THE STORY

APPENDIX B: PERFORMANCE WORKSHEET

OBJECT: *Who* am I talking to?

ACTION: *What* am I doing to them?

ENVIRONMENT: *Where* am I?

VALUES: *Why* am I doing this?

INTENTION: What do I *want*?

STAKES: What happens if I *succeed/fail*?

IDENTITY: Who am *I*?

RELATIONSHIP: Who are *we*?

HISTORY: How does the *past* affect the present?

IDENTIFY ALL MOMENTS OF CHANGE.
WHAT IS DIFFERENT BEFORE AND AFTER?

APPENDIX C: PERFORMANCE PLAN

Credit: Justin Miller

LYRIC	CHOREOGRAPHY *WHAT IS THE MOVE?*	PURPOSE *WHY ARE WE DOING IT?*

APPENDIX D: ON INHIBITION

It should be noted that this method is an evolutionary step, and as such, it assumes that choruses have already mastered the presentational method that has been the standard for decades. Sometimes there are performers that are totally new to performing altogether, that may be very inhibited and emotionally unavailable. For these singers, it may be appropriate to start with the older, presentational method of making everything big and exaggerated at first, to get them "out of their shell" and comfortable with on-stage expression.

To identify which performers are at this stage of development, we use the *Over The Top* exercise. The chorus is directed to perform a song without singing while going overboard on their expression—it should be cartoonish and ridiculous. Any performer who "goes too far" by successfully exaggerating their expression to ridiculous levels is pointed at, at which point they step off the risers. Soon, there will be only inhibited performers remaining whose idea of "too far" is actually not nearly far enough. Instead of looking huge, cartoonish and ridiculous, they still look inhibited, fearful, restrained, and small.

These performers need to recalibrate their internal barometer of what is "too much", so we ask them to perform the song again, and to keep exaggerating their performances, making them bigger and bigger until they get to the point where they are finally expressing themselves at a level appropriate to an on-stage performance. At that point, we say, "what you are doing now is not too big; you can be this big and it looks great." This usually is enough to recalibrate their sense of propriety and they will rapidly catch up to the rest of the chorus as their freedom of expression is no longer choked by fear.

Afterwards, we emphasize that *this is just an exercise!* It is by no means how we want to approach performance. It is explicitly and exclusively a way to move the internal barometer of what is "too much" so that the performer feels comfortable allowing their spontaneous, natural expression to have no limits. It helps to remove the fear that an impulse to move or express oneself is "too big" or will "stick out", because the performer has received explicit feedback that movements previously thought to be embarrassingly huge are, in fact, totally acceptable and appropriate.

APPENDIX E: BEYOND METHOD

In the context of evolutionary growth, it should be noted that this method is a step forward, not the end. The next stage of performance technique happens when the performer has become unconsciously competent with performance technique itself. At this stage, there is no longer a need to practice specific steps, or even to be aware of a structured performance process at all.

For a glimpse into what this level of artistry looks like, watch the documentary *Jim & Andy*, about Jim Carrey's transformation into Andy Kaufman for the movie *Man on the Moon*. Carrey said that he took the job, and from that point on, the spirit of Andy Kaufman took over. Carol Kaufman-Kerman, Andy Kaufman's sister, said of the experience "when he looked at me, I'm not kidding. [It was like] speaking to Andy from the great beyond" (Schonfeld, 2017, para. 4).

How does a performer get to this stage of artistic expression? There is no map. That's the whole point.

REFERENCES

Barr, T. (1997). *Acting for the camera.* New York, NY: Harper Collins.

Chekhov, M. (1993). *On the technique of acting.* New York, NY: Harper Collins.

Meisner, S., & Longwell, D. (1987). *Sanford Meisner on acting.* New York, NY: Vintage.

Morris, E., & Hotchkis, J. (2002) *No acting please: "Beyond the method" a revolutionary approach to acting and living.* Los Angeles, CA: Ermor.

Nachmanovitch, S. (1990) *Free play: Improvisation in life and art.* New York, NY: Penguin Putnam.

Schonfeld, Z. (2017, November 18). *I watched "Jim & Andy" with Andy Kaufman's brother and sister.* Retrieved from https://www.newsweek.com

Stanislavski, C. (1989). *An actor prepares.* London, UK: Taylor & Francis.

Winerman, L. (2005, October). The mind's mirror. *Monitor, 36*(9). Retrieved from https://www.apa.org/monitor

Wooten, V. (2006). *The music lesson: A spiritual search for growth through music.* New York, NY: Berkeley Books.

ABOUT THE AUTHOR

Micah Sloat has an Associate of Arts in Music Performance with Honors from Musician's Institute, where he studied guitar and voice. He graduated summa cum laude with a Bachelor of Arts in Philosophy from Skidmore College, and earned a Master of Arts in Transpersonal Psychology with a specialization in Creativity and Innovation from Sofia University. Sloat is a member of the Phi Beta Kappa and Phi Theta Kappa honor societies and is a lifetime member of MENSA.

A member of the Westminster Chorus for over 10 years, Sloat was onstage with the chorus for three BHS International Chorus Championship gold medal performances in 2010, 2015, and 2019 as well as the 2009 performances that won the Pavarotti Trophy and title of Choir of the World at the Llangollen Eisteddfod international music festival.

As an actor, Sloat is best known for his role in *Paranormal Activity*, a micro-budget horror film that broke box office records to become the most profitable film in history. *Paranormal Activity* launched a franchise with five sequels and nearly a billion dollars in box office sales.

As a certified Remote EMT, Sloat travels the world seeking adventure. He has climbed active volcanos in the Andes, paddled the entire coast of the Everglades National Park in a canoe, and trekked through the Amazon jungle to take part in the ancient ceremonial rituals of the indigenous tribes. He has a keen interest in esoteric spiritual practices and is a student of the Japanese battle arts.

www.ingramcontent.com/pod-product-compliance
Lightning Source LLC
Chambersburg PA
CBHW031614040426
42452CB00006B/510